# POEMS
# BY
# AN OLD CODGER

Book Five

44 Rhyming Poems from
World War 2 to COVID-19

NEIL DAVIES

Copyright @2023 Neil Davies

All rights reserved.

Independently published.

No part of this book can be reproduced in any form or written, electronic or mechanical, including photocopying, recording, or by any information retrieval system without written permission in writing by the author.

Although every precaution has been taken in the preparation of this book, the publisher and author assume no responsibility for errors or omissions. Neither is any liability assumed for damages resulting from the use of information contained herein.

*Dip in and enjoy,*
*Neil*

# MORE
## POEMS BY AN OLD CODGER
### WRITTEN BY NEIL DAVIES

Image by Ben Tattersall (Grandson)

# READERS' COMMENTS

## ON THE SERIES

- The number of poems written is truly wonderful, congratulations.

    K B Canada

- Joy to read.

    PW Bristol

- Congratulations, you're a poet as well as an old codger.

    G B London

- How talented you are.

    S R North Wales

- I laughed and I cried.

    M W North East Wales

# FOREWORD

Book Five provides a final contribution to the social history of the last century.

This book of 44 rhyming poems completes my personal reflections on the social history of the 20th Century, and an insight into aspects of my life influenced by tragedy and war.

The poems on growing up in a 'modern' mining village during war-time threats of invasion, rationing, military service, and the simple pleasures we enjoyed, may trigger memories for many elderly readers.

My personal observation on modern life are included in this series of over 180 rhyming poems

For younger readers, understanding all aspects of recent social history is essential. The step changes in lifestyle, travel, science, technology, medicine, and commerce, over my life time, have been greater, I believe, than any other similar period of time.

*Life moves fast. As much as you can, learn from your history, you have to move forward.*

Eddie Veddes

# CONTENTS

WHAT IS LOVE?

OLD CODGER'S OBSERVATIONS.

A GARDEN.

HOW IT WAS.

A POISONED CHALLICE.

MUSIC.

POLITICS IN CRISIS.

CARNIVAL TIME IN THE 'FIFTIES.

ON-LINE SHOPPING.

NEVER HAD IT SO GOOD.

VANDALISM AND HOOLIGANISM.

JOINT LOYALTY.

LOCKDOWN.

SOME RECOLLECTIONS FROM MY YOUTH.

COMMUNICATION.

ENERGY CRISIS.

MEMORIES OF SCHOOL DAYS.

AUTUMN IN THE COUNTRY.

SALUTE TO THE MINERS OF OLD.

PROVERBS 29 v18

INSTANT WORLD.

MINES RESCUE TEAMS.

DIVERSITY AND GENDER INDENTITY.

MODERN LIFE ON THE ROAD.

WALL OF REMEMBRANCE.

REFLECTIONS

A LOST VILLAGE.

BUTIN THE BADG.ER. - TWO YEARS ON.

WAR IS IMMINENT!

IN FOR REPAIR...

OUR AIR RAID SHE8LTER.

WAS I A CAT?

A STROLL DOWN MY OLD PLACE.

AMAZON RETAIL HEAVEN.

ODE TO WREXHAM TOWN.

THE DOCTOR CALLED.

TRIGEMINAL NEURALGIA

A SAD SIGHT.

GREAT GRANDFATHER & GREAT GRANDSON.

KEEP OLD MEMORIES ON THE SHELF.

BIRTH, LIFE AND DEATH.

## WHAT IS LOVE?

What is love which two living beings share,
And come together to form a pair.
Instant reaction, instant attraction,
Or a progressive friendship, a realisation.

A natural, comfortable, sense of bonding,
Absence triggering a heartfelt longing.
Amorous feeling, intense emotion,
A closeness that is more than affection.

A closeness that exceeds formality,
More than holding hands over a cup of tea.
Arm in arm, or closer still, just being together,
In love in all kinds of world-wide weather.

In sickness and in good health,
In hard times or with great wealth,
The bond-ship is tested and will always hold,
Even when both are growing old.

Many songs have been written
Of love and of someone smitten,
False interpretations of love, more like romance,
Light-hearted stories with music and dance.

Experts * have classified types of love as they must,
From friendship to passion, emotions to trust.
But for this Old Codger, I would guess
Love is surely mutual warmth, understanding,
and tenderness.

But the strongest love of all must be,
A mother's love for her new-born baby.

**000 - 000**

# AN OLD CODGER'S OBSERVATIONS

As I look around at these modern times,
I observe a host of deeply worrying signs.
And recall the Cenotaph words engraved
on a memorial display,
'For your tomorrow, we gave our today'*

Eighty years since those words were penned,
That 'tomorrow' is now today, my friend.
Was their gift worth all the sacrifice?
Were all those lives lost too great a price?

Eighty-five military invasions have occurred world-wide
Since 'Forty-Five'; it's international group genocide.
Life has become desensitised and vulgarised,
We have all become dehumanised.

Today the Queen's English is no longer cool,
Too many are talking in a dreadful, dreadful, drool.
And Grammar has been a victim of sloth,
My teacher would have gone into an almighty froth.

I cannot believe what I see on TV,
Thuggery, sex, and total nudity.
A false idea of love and beauty,
Influencing vulnerable minds is a form of cruelty.

The advances in technology, science, transport,
and health,
Have they improved a country's standards and wealth?

Often double-edged, with knock-on compensation to pay,
HS2's flattened properties; years of stored nuclear plant decay.

We've poisoned our earth, warmed up our planet,
Our irresponsible behaviour just "isn't cricket".
Space is littered with a spinning debris highway
And now we are seeking new frontiers so far away.

Let's consider all that's good,
Greater comfort, and a wider range of nutritious food.
Living longer, travelling to many far nations,
Education, health and safety regulations.

But this is not a world-wide situation,
There's hunger, poverty, violence, and starvation.
Nomadic lives seeking shelter and water courses,
Our world is still out of balance with its natural resources.

Can we claim 'our tomorrow' has met their sacrificial intention?
In truth, has life improved for any nation?
Have our priorities taken the wrong direction?
Will we ever achieve peace and perfection?

*John Maxwell Edmunds 1875 – 1958
Epitaph on the War Cemetery, Kohima.
"When you go home, tell them of us and say,
For your tomorrow, we gave our today"

**000 – 000**

# A GARDEN

If you are blessed with a garden space
It is a gift, not just an outside space.
However big or small, slim or wide,
Enjoy the land, treat it with respect and pride.

A haven for all its creatures to feed and hide,
From boundary and doorstep to the concrete curb-side.
For birds and bees, a source of food and water,
An open-air stage to gather, sing, and chatter.

When quenched, refreshed, and washed by rain,
Glistening leaves offer a reflective terrain.
Flowers turn their heads to the sun in the sky,
Enjoying the warmth as the day goes by.

A garden is a gymnasium for free,
A 'keep-fit' facility for you and me.
Lifting and stretching, bending, and stepping,
And a readily available free cup of tea.

Gardens, like cats, can have many a life,
A Kindergarten for mum and babe to thrive.
For toddlers to discover shadows and flowers,
Teenagers with bat and ball for hours and hours.

'Dig for Victory' was the wartime call,
A time of crisis for one and all.
If things get tough, money's not elastic,
Our gardens can help fill that empty basket.

So, plan your garden to suit your need,
Lawn for play, dug earth for seed,
Shrubs or plants, just follow the 'Gardener's Creed',
Don't let it stand there full of rubble and weed.

**ooo – ooo**

## HOW IT WAS

Dawn lights up this old terrace row,
Early morning traffic, some fast, some slow
Passes the window of one sleeping girl,
She stirs, the soft sheet revealing a human pearl.

She rises and lights the candle to hand,
Her flickering shadows creating a dancing dreamland.
It's cold, she quickly dresses in the candle-light,
Descends the stairs, a figure so slight.

Her father, home from night-time work,
The boiler lit, the kettle's on, he did not shirk.
The front room fire is young with little heat,
Gas mantle lights burn with a hissing bleat.

The boiler tap releases hot water to wash,
Carried over to the sink without a splash.
Lifebuoy soap, no privacy, so actions discrete,
Breakfast ready, hot porridge to eat.

Toilet calls often needed coat and hat,
A garden walk and a through-wall next-door chat
As one sits and ponders life staring at the T & G door,
Spaces top and low to vent any unpleasant odour.

Life was tough for this natural pearl to bear,
But she shone with rosy face and glorious hair.
Off to school, satchel conventionally brown and bright,
Holding homework written in her hand by candlelight.

Is this story about an era long ago?
A Dickens account of life so very low.
No! this ode recalls a more recent time,
It's about the Nineteen Fifties, truly,
offered up in rhyme.

**ooo – ooo**

# A POISONED CHALLICE

One Hundred and Sixty years or about that time
Alexandra Parkes created 'Parkesine'.
The world's first-ever, man-made, plastic state,
Then came polyethylene, polystyrene, nylon, plastic
clear or opaque.

Items in every colour, shape, and form,
Plastic parts in cars and throughout your home.
We welcomed plastic, thought it great,
But it's turned out to be a fatal threat.

It poisons our seas and the fish that in them swim,
Pollutes our rivers and fills almost everyone's weekly
bin.
We have opened a Pandora's Box of endless trouble
and more,
And I have expressed my concerns in print here
before**.

Single use plastics like food wrappers and bags,
Discarded in minutes but exists long after dusters and
rags.
Some good has evolved with many a new life saving
device,
But for all mankind it has become a poisoned chalice.

Moves are afoot to reduce the impact,
By encasing our goods as they are packed
In paper and cardboard rolled out in sheets,
Boxes to suit by clever origami techniques.

Cardboard boxes were originally part of head gear,
Lining men's hats to absorb sweat above the ear.
I am reminded of Pete Seeger's song about boxes *
As Amazon now floods my post with big and little boxes.

*It talks about
"people living in little boxes made of ticky tacky,
And they all go to university
And put in little boxes
And they all come out the same...."
Acknowledgement to Matvina Reynolds composer and singer 1962

** Book 2

**000 – 000**

# MUSIC

Music stirs the soul, the heart,
Whether you're together or apart.
Therapeutic for the anxious,
Every chord or note is precious.

Music stimulates, it raises the spirit,
It takes you out of any black deep pit.
It quells the fears, raises hope,
It's medicine that enables you to cope.

It tells a story from beginning to end,
Paints a picture as music notes blend.
Play it, sing it, why not write it
Or just listen and enjoy it.

Drink in the phrases,
The change in paces.
Drink in the harmony,
Enjoy the melody.

Forget your worries, leave the world,
Sit and absorb, grow warm not cold.
Let your mind dance whilst you sit on your seat,
Let your body swim with each wave or beat.

Let music be your buddy
When life is dark and muddy.
Let music lift your spirits high,
Renew your strength and your heart will fly.

Let music fill your space
With confidence and grace,
Banish your worrying thoughts and fears.
Let music brush away those tears.

Music paints so many scenes
Of life and love and builds your dreams.
It holds the key to your well-being,
Locks away any mental demon.

Music is a team event,
A blend of notes outward sent.
A marriage of instrument and player,
Notation created layer upon layer.

Music is as old as the hills,
Take it in and spit out those pills.
It's medicine in the purest form,
Helps to weather every storm.

Just wrap the music around yourself,
Leave your worries on the shelf.
The air vibrates, shakes off your fears
To soothe your mind and dry the tears.

**ooo – ooo**

## POLITICS IN CRISIS

All the Tories in the Shires
Fell a'sighing and sobbing so intent,
When they heard of the resigning
Of the latest Downing Street female resident.

Was the king-size bed too hard or just too soft,
Or the lounge too cold up high in the loft?
Was it that amplified demonstrator out on the street,
Or was it the thought of a self-inflicted party defeat?

The Socialist supporters cannot believe their luck,
They're dusting down their old manifesto book.
The Unions of every public service and more
Screaming for pay rises, to hell with the poor.

The Liberals and Greens are huddling together
To make up a pack, or is it just for the coming cold weather.
The devolved leaders are now all excited,
One's having a Cymraeg heart attack; Jock, the same old threat recited.

The media clan are gathering in an excited state,
Like seagulls around someone's meal on a plate,
Sly attacks as they swoop to destroy what's left,
Whilst you and I are both confused and bereft.

Enough is enough of this medieval governing throng,
With guaranteed payoffs, raised status, or 'Gong'.
It matters not if you're useless, stupid, or wrong,
So long as you toe the line and sing their song.

Spring Cleaning is urgently needed of House and member,
A modern replacement of building and every burnt ember.
Apply technology, communication, collaboration,
Stability in central governance and protect our nation.

**000 – 000**

## CARNIVAL TIME IN THE 'FIFTIES'

**A**rriving home from school one day,
Found my mother in a state of disarray.
Our lounge was full of large recording things,
Amplifier, microphone, loudspeakers, and cablings.

My father had ordered these from the Red Law company,
Famous film sound recording company known by many.
The Third Man, Jason and the Argonauts, and more,
Then, based in Manchester around Nineteen Fifty-Four.

Why were we housing this amplification lot?
Was my dad about to create the village nightclub spot?
Is he planning a new hobby or a retirement pastime?
No! it's the village's annual Carnival time.

When Father arrived home from work
Some explaining to do, he did not shirk.
He set about assembling the Kit,
When he finished, we had nowhere to sit.

He flicked the switch, microphone in hand,
Would it work and offer up a sound?
He tapped the mike and cleared his throat
And stood tall like a captain of his boat.

"Testing, Testing," came the call,
"One-a, two-a, three-a" the speakers' bawl.
The windows rattled, the doors shook,
Neighbours came out to take a look.

This post-war mining village annual festivity
Raised funds for the old folks' regular Christmas party.
Fancy-dressed folk came from far and wide,
Pearly Kings and Queens from as far as Merseyside.

Village Queens on decorated floats that raised the tone,
With their entourage sitting around the throne.
Morris Dancing groups, both senior and junior pals,
Competing for the championship cups and lots of medals.

My father realised, as applications came flooding in,
So many dancing groups meant a constant provision
Of music by the village colliery silver band until late,
But they were needed for the Carnival dancing date.

Now we knew why we were storing all this gear,
Having rocked the street and created neighbourhood fear.
But the best laid plans can come unstuck,
Father made a fundamental error and fell out of luck.

The Carnival proceeded through every colliery street,
Arriving at the Miners Welfare ground cut so neat.
A stage stood ready for the village Queen to be crowned,
And competitors lined-up ready for the judgement showdown.

The opening ceremony over, the dancing began,
A little while later my father began to implement his plan.

He switched on 'record' as the next troupe stood in alignment,
But as the band played on, he forgot,
and made an announcement.

"Will all the children come down from the stage."
was the request.
Alas, the announcement went out whenever the band took a rest,
And as nightfall approached it was a constant wasteless shout
As those keen Morris Dancers were still battling it out.

Village life, those post-war days,
Simple pleasures in so many ways.
Coming together to entertain and do their best,
Raising funds was their charitable quest.

**000 – 000**

## ON-LINE SHOPPING

Enough of trolleys and checkout queues,
Of heavy bags and shopping 'blues'.
We'll do our orders all at home,
Delivered by van, but soon by drone!

The list is long, the freezer's low,
An on-line order needs to go
To that market emporium all aglow,
With stocks so high and prices low.

I'll book a slot to suit the wife,
Choose the time and day to create no strife.
She needs to defrost and clean, you see,
Down to finding that last loose frozen pea.

The slot is booked, the rate is low,
Due on Monday, come rain or snow.
She gathers her list, it's 'in no particular order',
Influenced, I guess, by all the current TV fodder.

"Ham on the bone" she doth call,
I type in 'ham' and up come all.
Dry roast, boiled, and some with honey,
I click BUY, and the screen records the money.

"Cheese is next", the screen now full of processed curds,
Full fat, reduced fat, soft, mature, some with foreign words.
There's cottage, and cream, and jars with lemon,
'I'll order one we like that's very common.'

"Need potatoes" came the call from out of sight,
Sweet or seed, red or white?
Loose or bagged, chipped or mashed?
Large or small, grubby or washed?

The order arrived, the items reveal the truth,
Two dozen eggs, seven blocks of cheese,
four jars of marmalade, strewth!!
Three Bottles of bleach, boxes of cereals that cannot pass
through the cupboard door,
A sack of potatoes I cannot store.

Choices on screen are often many,
Various weights with various money.
The photographs are only part of the story,
There is no smell, no touch, no three-dimensional glory.

This multichoice game can be so confusing,
A psychological pattern is at play I'm thinking.
Stay focussed, stay on-line, do not sway,
Watch the account, don't be carried away.

**000 – 000**

## NEVER HAD IT SO GOOD

The words of Harold Macmillan,
Prime Minister and Earl of Stockton,
As the 'Fifties' made way for the 'Swinging Sixties'
Moving into an age of affluence with ease.

The 1950s was the time of recovery from war and loss,
Austerity, bomb sites, and human souls in chaos.
A militarised country, national service for most young men,
An indigenous nation soon to welcome multicultural citizens.

Victorian Sundays, class division, deadly smog, and pollution,
A threadbare, financially and morally exhausted nation.
'Rag and Bone Men', allotments to grow your family food,
Public transport plentiful, public telephones on selected corners stood.

Fifty million but few had cars,
Preservatives collected and stored in jars.
Near full employment it has to be said,
Marriage was the first time you met in bed.

Radio overtaken by BBC television's new public demand,
Surplus military bands offered up musicians
for many a dance band.

Victor Sylvester, Ted Heath and their orchestras,
and many more,
Enticing dancers young and old to take to the floor.

The age when singers of 'popular' music came along,
Frankie Vaughan with his "Green Door" song.
Tommy Steele 'Singing the Blues' and strumming his guitar,
Lita Rosa from Liverpool, Shirley Bassey became
a world-famous star.

Alma Cogan and her "Dream boat" song,
desiring kisses so much,
Jimmy Young and his "Unchained Melody"
hungered for 'her touch'.
Dicky Valentine's "Finger of Suspicion", died in a car
crash in Seventy-One,
Lonnie Donegan, King of Skiffle, and his "Pick a Bale of
Cotton" song.

Many of the static singers of that era, soon to be rejected,
As self-playing groups filled the stage
and movement was expected.
Economic expansion, buoyant state, as the space race
age began to emerge.
Macmillan's words reflect those latter years
of the Nineteen Fifty's page.

**000 -000**

# VANDALISM & HOOLIGANISM

This old codger when in short pants,
Collected old dead wood but never green plants
To build up a bonfire for Guy Fawkes night,
And one small box of fireworks to ignite.

The fireworks quickly pleased his gathered chums,
Bonfire embers cooked spuds and often fingers and thumbs.
The evening was young but the streets quite dark
So, it was considered time for a 'bit of a lark'.

Crouching at the end of a neighbours' gutter down pipe,
Stuffed up a sheet of newspaper and with one swipe
Struck a match, paper alight, and with a roar, up it went.
An element of hooliganism I now repent.

An annual night to celebrate the Gunpowder plot
To blow up the House of Lords, the King,
and that political lot.
Those post- war days when doors were open to all 'till dark
And streets were safe, no cars to park.

Growing affluence for some then spawned division and envy,
With loss of respect for people and property.
Creating reaction, rejection, unrest, disorder,
Criminal damage, hooliganism, to now adolescent murder.

No-one ever considered damaging a fence or public sign,
Steal lead from a church roof or washing on a line.
Never saw litter-strewn streets or seaside beach,
So, is there an absence now in what we teach?

Are our educational services fit for purpose, I ask?
Installing respect, obedience, and concentration in each task.
Are our training programmes ensuring pride and care prevails,
Developing high class essential vocational and social skills?

From little acorns oak trees grow,
Through bright sunshine and deep snow.
Their roots are sound, their branches strong,
All our young need to know right from wrong.

**000 – 000**

## JOINT LOYALTY

Oh Dear! what can the matter be?
Wales was beaten by a young full-back from Italy.
A swerving run, a sideslip or two,
This eleven-stone lad broke right through.

Joint loyalty must be our new duty,
Recognising all six nations' similarities and beauty,
The love of music, opera, and song,
Mountains and deep valleys stretching all along.

To those by Scottish Lochs and mountain tops,
With highland dress and whisky shops,
From Shetland to the Solway Firth,
A nation proud and 'down to earth'.

Kilt-less warriors wearing blue, with thistle on display,
Murrayfield, Flower of Scotland sung, and men ready to play.
Hastings, Townsend, Skinner, and Jonny Gray,
Always match fit and hoping to win on the day.

Across the Irish sea a united Ireland team for all can be seen,
Playing together, ranked number one in Twenty Nineteen.
Eleven players in the World Rugby Hall of Fame,
A young *Warren Gatland for three years coached their game!

Both anthems echo all around the ground,
What a truly significant, brotherly, sound.
Joint loyalty in music at Lansdowne Road,
A wonderful sporting message to behold.

Over the Channel at the Stade de France,
With the Golden Rooster of historical significance,
Is the home of their national rugby team,
With a hundred years of championship dream.

From the iron age Gauls to wars and revolutions,
France is now the world's leading tourist attraction.
It welcomes the games with the other five nations,
Providing a display packed full of emotions.

If only this union of nations was spread out from sport,
To eliminate those constant internal conflicts
of political retort.
And in the 'House' show loyalty, fidelity, and
dependability,
Not dishonesty, incompetency, inadequacy,
and constant snort.

*Wales coach 2008 – 2019. & 2023 - ?

**000 - 000**

# LOCKDOWN

Two years of constant lockdown
Has left me now with more than a frown.
Internment, my house an open prison,
And now I've become a different person.

Life-long daily order ceased,
Organised activities not released.
Cancelled plans and annual events,
Frustration and so many disappointments.

COVID lockdown nullified the spirit,
Affected so many human lives, I submit.
No desire to venture far
By foot or in my hybrid car.

Health and Care under constant strain,
As COVID spread across the plain.
Working under full protective cover,
Hoping it would soon all be over.

That critical phase of youthful days,
Vital to development in so many ways.
A lost chapter in the story of one's life,
An instigator of mental strife.

Social distancing still prevails,
Wearing masks to avoid all ills.
Going about in our reclaimed style,
But never close, never smile.

Nations' budgets up in the air,
Fighting the Bug, in a time of despair.
Emptied their chests, drained their pockets,
Now an era of borrowing, not of profits.

Whatever or whoever caused this catastrophe
Created a dreadful, world-wide, calamity.
Sorrow, fear, and great adversity,
Never again an act of such inhumanity.

**000 – 000**

## SOME RECOLLECTIONS FROM MY YOUTH

I recall the days when all cars were black,
And dogs lived in their kennels by the door at the back.
When personal transport was two-wheel pedal power
And a day trip to Blackpool, going up the Tower.

When coal was delivered in bags to the door
Or left loose on the road for miners to store.
A banana was a shape you coloured in yellow,
Dead chickens plucked and feathers collected for a pillow.

The cast iron Last to repair my boots and shoes,
The Lightman who called for the weekly dues.
One shilling for the electricity supplied by the Pit,
Carving knife sharpened, thrust into the garden grit.

Raffia table mats, home-made rugs lined with sacking,
Strips of coloured cloth pulled through by latch hooking.
Internal panelled doors covered by hardboard overlay,
Simple to paint, easy to clean, all for a small outlay.

Three-piece suites with fitted covers to suit,
Prolonging their life from dust and soot.
Curtain rails hidden by pelmets, colours to choose,
Fire guards fitted or just stood loose.

Old newspapers recycled whatever their state,
Under the kindling sticks to light the grate.
Pinned on the back of the toilet door nail,
Free bag of chips for a bundle to wrap up each shop sale.

The streetlight illuminated our nightly game,
Each evening was never the same.
We played with whatever we had,
Old tyres, cycle wheel rims, never disgruntled nor sad.

Spending more time outside than in,
The street our cricket pitch, football played with an empty tin.
Penknife a life-long friend; skipping ropes, single or double,
Enjoying our youth, never in trouble.

**000 – 000**

# COMMUNICATION

## *A Brief History of Mass Communication*

The history of mass communication
Goes way back to the days of an early nation,
When story telling was passed along
Just by voice or perhaps in song.

When fire was discovered by flint and kindling dry,
Damp shrub would produce smoke to rise up in the sky.
A form of signalling by puffed smoke was created,
To communicate far beyond where vocal sounds just dissipated.

From hill to hill and ship to ship, on demand,
Semaphore flags spelt out each command.
Then the Telegraph sent messages from land to land,
Morse code tapped out by each operator's hand.

When WW2 broke out, my father was trained in the code,
Sent to the hills of Burma, where a tent was his abode.
Instant communication from the 'Front' to 'Command'
As violent action was occurring across the land.

With landlines stretching across the country wide,
Under the sea and along mountain side,
The Telephone arrived on the street connected to the Exchange,
Housed in a red, windowed, unlocked kiosk, requiring loose change.

Coin boxes with buttons marked A and B to push
Press A when connection occurs; if not, press B, to retrieve your 'dosh'.
As a young scout, I was taught the language of semaphore,
And taken to practice on the village telephone with its very stiff door.

Homes and offices connected to the Exchange were next,
And Fax machines converted data to text.
Aerials on roofs brought radio and TV,
Now we could both listen and see.

In 1927, the BBC's motto as it opened its radio station
Was 'Nation shall speak peace unto Nation'.
Now mass communication has been developed beyond our dreams,
And speaking peace is lost in a world of marketing streams.

The internet arrived; mobile phones have shrunk to wristwatch size,
The world wide web was seen as a wonderful prize.
But digital communication today is overloading the mind,
Addictive, dominating, I am sure we'll all go blind.

This fingertip service has been hit by international hijackers,
By commercial media channels, bullies, and hackers.
We must seek protection of children and the vulnerable youth,
And especially protection of the truth.

**000 – 000**

# ENERGY CRISIS

Russian gas and Saudi oil,
Replacing coal miners' underground toil.
Our self-sufficient energy supply,
To that we said a foolish goodbye.

Fractional distillation,
Evaporation and condensation,
Providing petrol and diesel to take us far,
And camping gas to bitumen tar.

Now we have the new idea of fracking,
Will it cause earthquakes and house walls cracking?
When our coal mines were dug deep all around the place
The old tunnels collapsed creating surface subsidence.

For every action there will be a reaction,
So stated Newton as his third law of motion.
It applies more widely as ideas are challenged,
But our energy provision needs to be re-arranged.

Is it to be wind or is it tidal?
Nuclear, hydrogen, or solar panel?
Self-sufficient or become a subordinate state?
Hapless, helpless, we are moving far too late!

Decisiveness is what we need,
But Parliament will never take heed.
One cannot please everyone or every vocal group,
Follow professional advice or create more political soup.

The familiar political procrastination and debate,
Project criterions are placed at the starting gate,
Scientific, merit, management plan,
Budget, schedules, consultation, counterplan.

White papers, green papers, all required,
Developers frustrated; activists inspired.
U-turns, rumours, confusion abounds,
Another story for the media hounds.

Westminster press may now create an 'Energygate',
Associations with foreign leaders of an oil rich state.
Past misjudgements will come back to haunt you,
Leaving the public again to suffer and stew.

**000 - 000**

# MEMORIES OF SCHOOL DAYS

*"Let me have men around me that are fat*
*Sleek headed men who sleep o'nights,*
*Yon Cassius has a lean and hungry look;*
*He thinks too much:*
*Such men are dangerous."*

Ah! The only words I recall every day,
Not only sentiments triggered by our politicians' display
But instilled in me by violence and fear,
As I sat in class branded as group 5B.

The guy who taught us English Lit was short and lean,
Injured survivor of war, and what he'd seen
Like others, stayed with them all through later life,
And for us poor lads, periods of academic strife.

He paced the room delivering knowledge and fear,
Be prepared if he stopped quite near
And you are unable to utter what he wants to hear,
Lifted up by the short hair above your ear.

Well before we heard him come marching
down the corridor,
We sat in silence, in apprehension, hearts lying
on the floor.
Rule by fear is the way that Dictators hold on to power
But not in school, it turns learning sour.

As my wartime schooling started with my infant pupil band,
Our young men were all away defending our land.
It left elderly gents and matronly spinsters
With few resources and all fearing local bombing disasters.

Young ladies who entered the profession
Had a dilemma, a clash of passion.
Fall in love and so give up their teaching career,
Married women were not employed, causing many a tear.

Elderly spinsters' overweight, with perfume stale but sentimental,
In those wartime days they all carried the teaching mantle.
Rote Learning, blackboard, and chalk,
We listened and learned, ne'er dared to talk.

**000 - 000**

# AUTUMN IN THE COUNTRY

Michaelmas day, late September*, for years has stood
To honour the archangels three, so enjoy and do good.
Autumn's the time to gather together
The fruits that have endured our summer weather.

There's a chill in the air,
But do not despair.
Your labour and time have come bear,
The pantry is full for all to share.

Autumn leaves are starting to drop,
Enriching the land for next year's crop.
Red and brown, orange, and yellow,
Choose the land to now lie fallow.

Harvest Festivals and Halloween,
Witches and monsters, scariest ever seen.
Horse chestnut 'conkers' released from their casings,
Wait to be chosen and threaded with strings.

Bulbs for the Spring are laid in the soil,
Tools sharpened, a welcome break from gardening toil.
Catalogues scanned for next year's seeds,
Time to appreciate the year's good deeds.

Every year plans are a game of chance,
With frosts and drought challenging the romance
Of working with nature in all its forms,
Protection from searing heat and wild, wild storms.

There is a cycle to farming,
A cycle, too, with gardening,
Working in harmony or in strife
Just reflecting the cycle of life.

*29th September

**000 – 000**

## SALUTE TO MINERS OF OLD

Skill of hand, of pick, of shovel,
Growing their garden food with fork and trowel.
Who knew the rock that lay below,
And read the seams and what they show.

Men searched for coal with generous seams,
Trying to fulfil their wildest dreams.
With courage and faith beyond all measure,
They hacked at bedrock for 'black gold' pure.

Lined mining shafts began in Tudor times with no plan,
Technology, Health and Safety, were non-existent aids for man.
Black damp, flooding, gas of unknown extent,
Basket tubs of coal, hooked to rope, upward sent.

When a seam of coal was thought to exist below,
A 'Bell Pit' was dug, earth spoil bagged, sent up by tow.
A 'horse-gin'*, powered by circulating horse and rope,
How big and rich is this find, to give them hope?

Both coal and stones arrived on top,
Horse drawn wagons are loaded with the initial crop.
Concessionary coal for miners' homes,
Before the rest was screened of stones.

When times were tough, no work for many a week,
Men dug down deep in their gardens to seek
A chance encounter with that source of heat.
Tenacity, desperation, as poverty they tried to beat.

A group of small working mines where miners' toll,
Offered another approach to find the run of coal.
Into the side of a nearby hill, drift mines were cut,
A couple of mates with basic tools and a storage hut.

Over the years, mines, large and small, have lost their soul,
Politics and economics the demise of our British coal.
The end is nigh; in 'Twenty-Four' the last miners will end their toll,
As power stations turn their back on our British coal.

Over three hundred years, that's back some way,
Men, boys, and ponies have toiled away
In those dark, damp, noisy stations.
An 'Ask' above and beyond all other vocations.

Times not knowing if there was work or not,
Times when conditions were unbearably hot.
Times not knowing if life would end with a spark,
And never again hear the singing of the morning Lark.

Miners bore the signs of their work without and within,
Black splinters embedded in their skin.
Family men when washed off the filth,
Who gave their life, gave their health, for little wealth.
* Type of Windlass.

# PROVERBS 29 v18

*"Where there is no vision,
the people perish:
but he that keepeth the law,
happy is he."*

*\*A man without a vision
Is a man without a future,
A man without a future
Will always return to his past.*

Proverbs is a 'Wisdom Book' in the Hebrew scriptures,
Wise sayings offering guidance and values, with no pictures,
Meaning of life, of conduct and behaviour,
and the art of living.
The 'Wikipedia' of today that is being offered free to every human being.

Proverbs, twenty-nine, verse eighteen, a modern translation, *
Relates to many an old Codger's cogitation,
With time to think, reflect, recall,
Of earlier times and personal incidents both large and small.

The words above encourage all to follow their dream,
To strike out alone or be part of a team.
Set yourself an aim, stay focussed, do not be distracted,
And you will never end up broken hearted.

A man without a future
May never leave his past.
But this old Codger has enjoyed much of life's adventure,
And can now sit and ruminate at last.

**000 - 000**

# INSTANT WORLD

Instant coffee, instant tea,
Instant custard for you and for me.

Instant meals, frozen chips,
'Three For Two' to widen the hips.

Instant beans, instant peas, instant salads,
Instant fruit for all those healthy lads.

Instant food in every store,
Not seasonal produce anymore.

Instant light, just a switch to flick,
Instant heat, no coal nor stick.

Instant water, hot or cold,
Instant flow, a trickle or bold.

Instant journeys if you have a car
To travel near or travel far.

Instant contact between friends with ease,
Instant news from across the seas.

Instant photos, instant films,
Instant 'selfies' of 'hers' and 'hims'.

Instant shopping but not in shops,
Instant orders on phones or laptops.

Our instantaneous expectation
Is met by retailers across our nation.

Not so our beleaguered NHS,
Overwhelmed and now full of stress.

No instant appointments for diagnosis
By phone nor at their premises.

Our politicians just prevaricate,
We are heading for an "Instantgate".

"A Working Party", "An Inquiry",
"Fix a Debate date in our diary".

They'll set up a sub-committee of a committee,
That reports to a Junior Minister,
who reports to his/her Ministerial MP.

We've lost our patience, our tolerance is low,
One instant world, another running slow.

**000 -000**

## COAL MINES RESCUE TEAMS

Men of great courage and special grit,
When called, stepped forward to descend their broken pit.
Never faulted, trained to rescue their fellow men,
Not knowing what was waiting in that deep black den.

· A Rescue Team of Captain and six trained men
Stand prepared to do their job, accept their burden.
Find their friends trapped or lying down below,
The cage descends, the gates are opened slow.

What will they encounter as they leave the cage?
For the life of the mine, is this its last page?
Bodies rigid, bodies bleeding, in the dark,
The scene before them may be quite stark.

They know the drill as they go into gear,
Steady their nerves, hold back their fear.
Is there air supporting fire? Is there gas?
A roof fall blocking any means to pass.

Is there life, a moan, a structural groan,
Rescuing is the job they own.
To save a life can be a challenge too far,
But success should be a Medal and Bar.

**000 - 000**

In memory of Thomas Henry Jones, aged 28, Uncle.

Killed whist attempting rescue following mine explosion and fire at Holditch Colliery (Known as The Brymbo Pit), 1937.

## DIVERSITY AND GENDER IDENTITY

There is a need to recognise universal diversity,
If we are to embrace this international complexity,
With so many dimensions to this reality,
From language, culture to sexuality.

All are steeped in social history,
An understanding of diverse societies
Is a challenge to navigate and embrace,
When locked in one life, one place.

Do our brains develop neurodiversity,
Enabling tolerance and empathy,
And help navigate a life of harmony,
Eliminating violence and tyranny.

----------

*"I'm not sure if I am a 'her' or 'he',
Perhaps I need some therapy,
Or even undergo plastic surgery
I guess I'll just have to wait and see."*

Gender identity and reassignment
Can be a major life-changing event,
From Music Hall drag to surgeon's knife,
From a husband to a newly formed wife.

From wearing make-up or visa-versa,
Change in dress and vocals 'coarser'.

To a human's new permanent state,
No going back, it's now too late.

Is there a line to draw,
Where surgery has to be the very last straw,
Where genderqueer is intolerable,
And re-assignment makes life more comfortable.

Or are we seeing a fad like tattooing,
Plastic surgery for cosmetic enhancing.
Attention seeking, depressed or bored,
Has this gender identity been fully explored?

**000 – 000**

## MODERN LIFE ON THE ROAD

Traffic calming high raised strips of tarmac
Taken many an exhaust pipe and human back.
Damaging tyres, corded edges left in shreds,
Suspensions weakened and stripped bolt threads.

Because of a few selfish law-defying motorists,
Ignore the highway code, blatant non-conformists.
Law abiding motorists obliged to daily mount these hurdles,
And as I do, my blood just curdles.

Tailgating, undertaking, alcoholic and drugged-up eyes,
Souped up cars, altered bore and piston size.
Noisy exhausts to pierce one's ears,
Showing off to their moron peers.

There are laws to stop this, but what an ask
Enforcing them is an impossible task.
Policing them is a thankless job,
Lenient penalties, petty fines of just a few 'Bob'.

We are all God's Children, so they say,
But there are those who got away.
Joined the Devil and all his dealings,
Living a life as his selfish siblings.

Our roads are littered with humps and signs,
Cycle tracks and painted lines.
The Highway Code spells it out,
Never read by any motoring lout.

"You are driving a killer machine,"
Said my instructor, and he was keen
To press it home and make the point.
So lay off drink and give up the 'joint'.

No insurance nor tax, for their auto,
Tyres not checked, but away they go.
To be driving they have an embargo,
Each a dangerous motoring rogue.

I pray for a time we never chance to meet
These inconsiderate people motoring along on any street.
No care for others, enjoying their noisy radio soiree,
Just lock them up and lose the key.

**000 - 000**

# WALL OF REMEMBRANCE

A wall of bricks bearing each miner's name,
A wall of remembrance, a wall of shame,
A wall that's gathered all the men together,
Companionship in stone, friendship for ever.

A list so long, all killed at their post,
Sweating as they toiled, bodies hot as toast.
A wall so stark, so many lost souls,
Where they lived, their age, their roles.

Working a two- hundred yard long coal face
That night, a very dangerous, dreadful place.
A stifling, dusty, choking den,
Fiery heat, and almost naked men.

They worked that Dennis Deep in daily fear,
To feed their families held so dear.
Many worked a double shift that night,
The Carnival's in town, so a day of delight.

A time when miners' morale was at rock bottom,
And high unemployment, so life was truly rotten.
That double shift was encouraged by the bosses,
To reach their Quotas, avoiding financial losses.

166 widows, 241 children and 209 dependents,
Devoid of their love, protection, and precious moments.
Devoid of bread on the table, of heat in the grate,
And the rent man will be coming through the garden gate.

The tomb was sealed, the records lost,
Excavating coal was at any cost.
Those miners had punched holes in their soles,
To drain the sweat from feet and toes.

No bodies to carry up into that September light,
No grave to visit or lay them right,
No way of saying a last farewell,
They lie together in a place like Hell.

Shoulder to shoulder for that black gold,
Those men and boys will never grow old.
At two in the morning, they died together,
This wall, a memorial for us all to remember.

*In memory of John Robert Jones (Grandfather/Taid)

1879 - 1934

**000 – 000**

The Wall of Remembrance at the Miners' Rescue Station.

# REFLECTIONS

Oh dear! I'm now down to a slim fit size,
Disappearing hair and overworked eyes.
Having to shave between each facial line,
I look like 'Compo', another 'last of the summer wine.'

I have now lost track of the days of the week,
It's Friday when the bin men arrive, my bins they seek.
A weekly event happening far too quick,
I guess I will also soon be needing a stick.

I fumble and stumble and get in a stew,
I'm growing more and more like Victor Meldrew.
I cannot believe what I see on TV,
Thuggery, sex, and total nudity.

My hearing suggests the Queen's English is no longer cool,
Too many are talking in a dreadful, dreadful, drool.
And Grammar has been a victim of sloth,
My teacher would have gone into an almighty froth.

My memory is in a complex state,
Why have I just walked down to the garden gate?
I can remember my teachers' names of long ago,
But not when I go shopping at my local convenience store.

Modern life is not for me,
Clutching phones or plastic cups of instant coffee.
Dashing along in a frantic hurry,
Or squatting to devour cartons of spiced up curry.

There's nothing new in this revelation,
It's happened to many across the nation.
When Old Father Time comes a'knocking,
The truth can be quite stark and shocking.

But I've been standing since just after I was born,
I've weathered some challenges and many a storm,
World-wide terror and today's worrying political activity,
So, I'll just keep smiling, and book my annual MOT.?

**ooo – ooo**

# A LOST VILLAGE

Returning to my dear seaside village,
It looks as if it's all been pillaged.
The weather now has turned quite cold,
Houses claiming "SOLD", "SOLD", "SOLD".

The street is quiet, empty, the air is still,
Where I played football improving my skill.
Watched by our dads, leaning over their walls or gates,
Whilst the young sat devouring a 'Butty' on a plate.

What has happened to my village street?
The fishing boats are all deplete.
Expensive yachts, sheets clanging like a one-piece band.
Wrapped up, lying in water or the dry dock land.

There's big money along the harbour on show,
I guess our fishing trade has taken a blow.
The corner shop, where my old mum had daily chats,
Expanded into a pair of luxury holiday flats.

Passing my old village school, in need of repair,
Council notice declaring 'Planned Closure, Go Elsewhere'
A village without the sound of children at play
Is just a hamlet, demoralized, in decay.

Come the Spring, warmer weather,
It's a false village as temporary people gather.
Four by Fours arrive with wine and food,
Not a community, it's not even a neighbourhood.

A village that's stark for half a year,
Endured by its residents, the young shedding a tear.
More strangers re-appear as days do lengthen,
To 'camp' in their bricks and mortar, aside the village brethren.

It's a summer base away from the smoke,
Living in our houses now bespoke.
To enjoy our air, the sea, sometimes the weather,
Local couples hapless, at the end of their tether.

Is it a desire to seek our waterside sun?
To relax, recharge, and have some fun
Or a financial investment, make more dosh?
For the community, it's a total loss.

Or to talk of their summer retreat by the sea
Back home, with friends, supping 'orange pekoe' tea.
What summer sales the villagers make, with little cheer,
It's not enough to buy even a crate of local winter beer.

The doors of our homes were never closed,
No-one's entry was ever opposed.
Holiday houses in my street are now heavily secure,
Shuttered, bolted, alarmed, no doubt heavily insured!

I would like to sow a little seed,
A Holiday Chalet should meet your need.
They're large and grand along the top of the beach
And keep your capital where the taxman can't reach.

Live in your yachts at the Quay or a mooring,
Stop gazumping our local young lovers, they're so alluring.
Just pack up and leave and heed my suggestion,
Stop changing village life and creating traffic congestion.

**000 - 000**

## BUTIN THE BADGER – TWO YEARS ON

**B**utin the badger's incursions, before the light of dawn
Crosses the border attacking our lawn.
I have already told of his nightly visits,*
Whilst we were in Lockdown, he scored many hits.

I've used bricks and sticks,
Netting and slabs to no avail,
I dare not harm this carrier of bugs and ticks,
Or I will end up in the local jail.

I've plenty of film of this mighty 'Hood',
Digging up my lawn in search of food.
Striding around like he owns the place,
Faces the camera like a Hollywood ace.

Chemical warfare I have now let loose,
Sprayed my boundary with badger resistant juice.
The smell in the garden has gone to my head,
It still lingers on my clothes and in my shed.

Oh! Now he's changed his military tack,
It's an Eastern front trellis advancing attack.
Chewed a spar or two to enter through,
He's pulled back from his rear garden view.

I need reinforcements from city hall,
Or a rate review, if they'll play ball.
Or perhaps an "Autumn Watch" series on the 'Tele',
Well, I've already filmed him scratching his belly.

I must confess that I am beat,
The game is ending in defeat.
My nightly visitor has worn me down,
I've been blocking holes like a demented clown.

It needs a peace treaty put in place,
Neither party has failed nor in disgrace.
Nature has taught this old codger
Love thy neighbour and this black and white lodger.

*See:  Poems by an Old Codger – Book 4

**000 – 000**

## WAR IS IMMINENT! - 2020

The forces are gathering on Offa's Dyke,
Our First Minister has mounted his bike.
Like the dragon of old, hot air has been blown,
English beware, don't try to enter, stay home.

We don't want your bugs, we do miss your cash,
You could creep over and then make dash,
And hide in a cave or old mine shaft,
If you are caught, just pretend to be daft.

There are many who are, in this land of song,
And holding office for far too long,
Gird your loins, mask your face,
There's plenty of room in our mountainous space.

Cross the Dee or Severn, use a boat with pedals,
Or carve a route along the Newport levels.
Boris needs a scout or two down there,
He's raring to go; poor First Minister is tearing his hair.

There was a time when, in reverse order,
Sunday coachloads would slip over the border
To sup the beer from English hops,
Chapels were open but no pubs or shops.

So! fear not, all you locked up in John Bull land,
A favour needs repaying, our beer is quite grand.
Time your move, as at closing time they gather,
If stopped, just say "Lloyd George knew my father".

# IN FOR REPAIR

My laptop has had to go in for repair,
I don't think it's due to fair wear and tear.
Someone has hacked in with evil intent,
If caught, to prison they should be sent.

The Boiler's lost pressure, I'll do an inspection,
Is there a leak or it just needs attention?
I'm advised to seek YouTube for guidance and care,
But my laptop has gone in for urgent repair.

I sent an email before the 'hack' took place,
Hoping for a prompt reply, back in haste.
It may have been sent and lies in the air,
Because my laptop has gone in for urgent repair.

My phone is the lifeline in this situation,
This miniature laptop is carried by almost the nation.
I'll keep it charged up as a handy spare,
As my laptop has gone in for urgent repair.

'When will my books come?' asks my patient dear wife,
With no books to read, she's heading for strife.
"My phone has no messages" I tenderly declare,
My laptop, dear, has gone in for urgent repair.

My desk now looks quite empty and bare
As at the empty socket I ponder and stare.
When I collect my machine and ease my despair.
What will be the cost of my Acer gone in for repair?

The expert explained that no hacking occurred,
"I've found the problem", the guy smiled and purred.
"Your Hard Drive was failing, no evil affair,
Bring in your laptop if you ever need another repair".

**000 – 000**

# OUR AIR RAID SHELTER

As war was imminent in early 'Thirty-Nine,
A safe shelter for everyone was prime.
Urban mass shelters in any public Underground,
Options for individual families needed to be found.

Morrison steel shelters, assemble in the home,
Table-like, occupying almost the whole living room.
Anderson garden shelters dug four feet deep,
Where occupants were expected to sleep.

My Nain's sons and mining pals stepped in with a plan,
Dug a large deep oblong hole in the garden.
Six steps down, bricked all around: a mini land grab,
Covered with a row of precast curved concrete slab.

This Stanton type shelter took pride of place,
If Gerry came over there would be a race
To get down below into this dark damp shelter.
Sturdy idea, prominently placed, it was a belter.

Sadly, this haven was condemned by the shelter man,
Never to be used in time of an air alarm.
It stood aloof and alone until one day
When a little boy found a new place to play.

It became a submarine at sea, a dark den,
A damp floor and spare house bricks, about ten.
War ended and left with this obsolete garden 'ornament'
Thoughts of growing mushrooms, but with no intent.

It served to raise this young lad's view,
Over the hedge and across the valley too.
It was still there when this chap went away,
This icon of war was still holding sway.

Those wailing sirens across the Ukrainian capital,
Flipped me back to our wartime orders quite regimental.
The approaching bombers are coming in from the West,
Pit head siren, total blackout, for protection we did our best.

An episode in my early life,
Prompted by the current European strife.
I recall the fear as the enemy flew overhead,
Mother and I under the stairs, Nain lying in her bed.

This new abhorrent act on the world-wide stage,
For the history books another page.
A violent attack on one's closest neighbour,
Actions I cannot understand nor savour.

A despot who by means illegal and devious,
With cronies, and 'Yes' men, supporting his actions so serious,
Has turned peace and friendship into violation,
They all need to be eradicated by their nation.

**000 – 000**

# WAS I A CAT?

In my previous life I was a cat,
I'm nodding off daily but not on the mat.
So says my wife, a font of all knowledge,
But I do not scratch nor sit on the window ledge.

My wife is keen to serve me lots of fish
On a plate not in a dish.
Is it Whiskas, Felix or Kittie- Kat
Or to stop me getting fat?

Have I had a previous life?
This suggestion by my wife
Made me think she may be right,
De je Vu triggered by a place or sight.

Is it one's previous life or is it ancestry triggering
A feeling of being here before, that's niggling.
Reincarnation? Or is it in our genes,
That carries forward familiar scenes.

We all have a past, perhaps not a previous life,
Influenced by those who came before and laid our genes.
Is it in our blood, passed down through our ancestors'
high or low life?
Is that why we are confused when we recognise new
places or scenes.

It may be music, it may be smells,
Or the ringing of an old church bells.
A feeling, a habit, carried through from our family long gone.
That we are now privileged to share from days bygone.

I'll leave you with these thoughts and my troubled brow,
And go find the cat flap and grit tray now.
Smarten myself up ready for my night-time foray,
And leave a mouse or two on the wife's breakfast tray.

**000 – 000**

## A STROLL DOWN MY OLD PLACE

As night follows day,
Every Sunday a group came to pray,
And sing hymns outside our house.
They gathered, their message to espouse.

With tambourines and shiny accordion,
They sought to convert the local ruffian.
'Repent' they yelled; 'Be Forgiven',
Or our life was about to be quite riven.

My father away at war, not Europe, the forgotten other,
My mother, housebound, nursing her bedridden mother,
As their amplified call to 'Come and meet your Saviour',
My mother loudly suggested they came in and
nursed her mother.

It was a modern, quiet, council street,
Uncluttered roads, regularly cleaned, gardens quite neat.
Regularly maintained by steam roller and tar,
Housing miners, heaving out coal to support the war.

Some time ago I made the mistake of revisiting my
street,
Bringing back those memories of my playground beat.
Alas, my heart was broken, and I was in dismay,
Signs of hardship, poverty, and decay.

My play street now lined with an array of old cars
And an image of decline and visual scars.
Graffiti sprayed along my old garden wall,
A local source of drugs was its call.

Like those saplings on the Alyn valley wall,
That now have grown so wide and tall,
Time has changed the nature of my street,
A place of harmony to one deplete.

Seventy years on. my street looked strange,
A reflection of the impact of industrial change.
A guarantee of village mining work all gone,
Hard manual work no longer required from anyone.

My street is just one of many, I'm sure,
Once rich in life, but now no more.
We lived in concord, friendship, and mutual respect,
But our new world is causing a damaging social effect.

**000 – 000**

## AMAZON RETAIL HEAVEN

Let your fingers do the shopping,
At your desk, not town shop hopping.
A one-stop screen, a comfortable chair,
Take a break, a stroll out in the fresh air.

Let your fingers do the shopping,
A driver's soon on the way, doorstep dropping.
Seven-day service rain or sun,
Even third-party sellers sell on Amazon.

Let your fingers do the shopping,
This on-line market sells just everything.
A disruptor of traditional retail life,
Leaving shops in grief and strife.

Let your finger do the shopping,
Every item under the sun is beckoning,
Using an E-commerce platform space
Has produced this on-line marketplace.

Finger shopping is not new to me,
Catalogue shopping over a cup of tea.
Books, thick as the Bible, dropped at the doors,
Passed around, agents then collected the orders.

Finger shopping is so addictive and time consumable,
Personal stored history means items offered are predictable.
Cannot touch, smell, or taste,
Orders placed in too much haste.

It all started, selling books, Colorado, '98,
Every commodity and more, is on their 'slate'.
Every market has been incorporated into their chain,
No product 'stone' has not been turned to their gain.

Shopping as we know it has gone away,
And 'takeaways' are holding sway.
African 'rap' has a world-wide call,
Young ladies are now playing professional football!

Amazon reflects our changing world,
Their development has been quite bold.
Instant reaction to instant demand,
We must not bury our heads in a sinking sand.

**000 – 000**

## ODE TO WREXHAM TOWN

My old town, just received City status,
Having served our applications and with patience.
This old town existing from pre-Roman times,
Excavation has provided many interesting finds.

Nearby Borras* held Mesolitic man's flint implements,
Perhaps I should dig deep, forget my garden plants.
Oh! I guess I would look a right proper chump,
This land was once the old town's rubbish dump.

Medieval fairs replaced by market traders and their wares,
This market town a regional centre as the Civil War flares.
Witnessed on nearby Holt village church walls
Are the marks from an array of the conflicts' cannon balls.

A market town, a thriving place, and ample water to share,
Leather by skinners and tanners, horns for buttons, combs for hair.
Ruabon bricks, built homes across the nation,
Wrexham Lager travelled far by reputation.

'Iron Mad' Wilkinson's ironworks in Seventeen Sixty-Two,
The industrial revolution then arrived here too.
A thirsty environment, beer to pass working man's dry lips,
Almost twenty breweries in the two linked townships. **

My old town has been turned around,
Gone the mines, no more working underground.
Technology has provided employment succour,
Gone the need for manual labour.

The footprint of this new border city,
Expanding and consuming land of necessity.
Homes for the young is a major priority,
So too, the need for good care and prosperity.

My old town has always been a friendly place,
Full of hospitality, charm, and grace,
It's now a cosmopolitan, multi-language, multi-cultural city
Developing a progressive new identity.

A new investment to boost our beating heartland,
Once the 'Wrexham Robins' FC, with an ash bank 'stand'.
Now the prospect of great things to come,
For a bustling city I call home.

*East edge of town.
** Wrexham Abbot originally belonging to the Church (e g. Abbot street),
Wrexham Regis originally answered to the King (e g. King Street)

## THE DOCTOR CALLED

'Take your shoes off and come into the house.'
He steps inside like a timid church mouse.
'Hang your coat on the nearest peg,
Oh! there is a patch of mud on your trouser leg.'

'Take a seat on that old Windsor chair,
It used to be one of an antique pair.
Thanks for coming, I've waited long,
I'm sure my exercises are all wrong.'

'I do them every day for sure,
But I'm still seeking a perfect cure.
I need to stand up straight, shoulders back,
I don't want to look like an old potato sack.'

'My voice is rough, my chest is tight,
My breathing is still not quite right.
My hair is thin and falling out,
And my big toe has now developed gout.'

'I cannot touch my toes no more
And my heels have now become very sore.
I totter as my balance goes awry,
At times I almost want to cry.'

'I'm so glad that you could call,
I'm almost climbing up the kitchen wall.
I've telephoned the early morning request,
Ten times I failed, at least I've done my best.'

*Well, my dear, you must see*
*It's all about our economy.*
*Younger chaps have left, gone overseas,*
*And the rest of us are on our knees.*

*Remember when our Health Minister tweaked,*
*Raised our salary and shortened our week.*
*She's long since gone to the Upper House*
*To enjoy a plate of Lancashire 'Scouse.*

*The NHS is overwhelmed and fraught,*
*Your treatment will soon have to be bought.*
*Put the kettle on and make a pot of tea,*
*And then I'll give you a thorough MOT.*

"Wake up! Gran, you do look pale
Have you been drinking that local ale?".
'I dreamt my doctor called to see me,
Long time ago that's what happened, you see.'

**000 – 000**

## TRIGEMINAL NEURALGIA

A silent attack, a silent stab,
So violent I needed something to grab.
No warning, it came right out of the blue,
I hope it never ever happens to you.

It was a Christmas Eve as I prepared for bed,
A seasonal present it has to be said,
But not one that I would wish to spread,
It seems I have a problematic head.

The problem is we're not quite sure,
A diagnosis is needed that is sound and pure
Of what exactly triggers the nerve and pain,
That splits around the face having come from near the brain.

A blood vessel presses on the protective nerve's myelin sheath
And in time may wear it away, that's a very strong belief.
But this does not explain the quiet periods of relief,
Which can last for weeks or months then gives you grief.

The three nerve endings under the face's skin
Can lie in a state of quiet but excited strain,
Triggered into attack by brushing your teeth or smiling,
Shaving, swallowing, chewing, and even kissing!

My heart goes out to those who's daily life
Is frequent attacks and constant strife,
Held at bay by a cocktail of pills
Considering the option of surgeons' skills.

I lay my thoughts as an intermittent suffering guy,
Noting the lack of public attention to our cry
For increased research and understanding
Of this silent illness so damned debilitating.

(**N.B.** Anyone who suffers from this condition may wish to consider joining the Trigeminal Neuralgia Association).

**000 – 000**

## A SAD SIGHT **

Stud in tongue, ring in nose,
There she sat in quiet repose.
Safety pins through each ear,
"Have you got a fag, for this poor dear?"

Tattooed arms covering well-worn flesh,
Hair tied back in an old black silk mesh.
Well-worn daps tied with string,
Blue veined legs with scratches that must sting.

An old grey cardigan that has lost its shape,
Missing buttons and holes that gape.
Her pleated skirt has seen better days,
Stained by food consumed in unusual ways.

Tobacco-stained fingers that tremble and shake,
Stretching out wide for tea and cake
As she used to enjoy in her place of care,
But now receives just the occasional stare.

Her well-worn bag of unknown possessions,
Supports her back during these daily sessions.
Squatting up against an office wall,
Where cats and dogs have left their call.

This bag lady is not alone on any street,
Take a stroll day or night and you will meet
Homeless, hapless, luckless human beings,
Love lost, neglected, rejected, no finger rings.

How can so many sink so low?
A life and living that drags on so slow.
A future with no care, no horizons,
For them our streets are just open prisons.

Is it a follow-on from child neglect,
Or no-one around to guide and protect?
Wrong company, trauma, mental stress,
Addiction, loss, or from living under duress?

A slippery path that leads nowhere
But crime, ill health, and no-one to share,
To understand, maintain support, turn it around,
Alas, no choice but to beg and sleep on the ground.

\*\* A compilation of street dwellers

**000 – 000**

## GREAT GRANDFATHER AND GREAT GRANDSON

Reached old age,
A new-born page.

Tired out and slow,
Keen to be on the go.

Failing teeth to eat,
Cutting teeth so neat.

Fading sight to see,
Seeing life with glee.

Lined and well-worn skin,
Statin soft like brand new linen.

A life-time experience of peace and warring,
An innocent child with no life's scarring.

Wary of all and sundry,
Trusting, relying, knows no boundary.

Wonderful family and friends for life,
So, grow up strong and find a good wife.

*For Joey.

**000 – 000**

## KEEP OLD MEMORIES ON THE SHELF

Started life with straight teeth and curly hair,
Now it's missing teeth and a head going bare.
Learned to walk with a push-along stuffed dog,
Now I shuffle like I've had too much grog.

Symbols of change over eighty years,
Life and time, laughter, and tears,
Wear and tear, disappointments, and fears,
An impact on the human frame thus appears.

Whilst the heart and spirit may soldier on
The mind and soul are like an old song.
Everlasting words and hypnotic tunes so bold
Provide a constant link with times of old.

These memories are personal, individual, unique,
The young will consider them quite antique.
So why should we talk of our younger days,
The world will never stage a run of replays.

Memories only provide a segment, a sliver, a gaze
Of personal life as we recall those early days,
Living within a wartime, stressful, working nation,
An imbalance on the total world situation.

Our world has always been in a degree of stress,
Man-made conflicts generating many a human mess.
Man survives by looking ahead with innovation,
Not looking back in self adoration.

Life moves on to handle change that's good or bad,
This old codger must stop complaining and feeling sad.
Keep my thoughts and memories to myself,
Let them all lie on that dusty garden shed shelf.

**000 – 000**

# BIRTH, LIFE AND DEATH

## BIRTH

Celebrations abound as we alight,
With baggage so little and so light,
Onto the ever-flowing escalator of life
As it moves us all through harmony and strife.

We cry as soon as we arrive on earth,
We learn to smile soon after birth.
We crawl, we stand, just feeling grand,
We walk upright across the land.

## LIFE

Pre-school hours offer friendship and sharing,
Then on to the formal era of learning,
Of discipline, success, and failure,
The reality of life and elements of danger.

It's a personal individual path one treads,
Until one meets another and subsequently weds.
The path gets wider, hearts get torn,
Responsibilities and care must now be borne.

## DEATH

The span of life is unknown,
The quality of life you can own
Recreation, family, and good strong friendship
Happiness, comfort, or pain and hardship.

The only certainty whilst on this earth
Is that our end will come some time from birth.
Whilst many plants can sleep and then regrow,
We live expecting we'll still be here tomorrow.

*Do not cry, don't be sad,*
*Remember my life, of which I'm glad.*
*So, raise a glass it's hereby written,*
*To an absent friend ne'er to be forgotten.*
(Author)

# EPILOGUE

# A Review of COVID - 19

# A REVIEW OF COVID-19 – 1

## Observations on the event.

Did we close our borders too late,
To hold back travellers but not our freight.
Did our quarantine have its effect,
The urgent need our population to protect.

What has this virus done to us all,
Were we ready to meet the call?
How well did we know the strain of the bug?
Warned to neither kiss nor hug.

An already creaking NHS with little to spare,
Providers of Care a poisoned chalice to bear.
Planned treatment shelved, attention to a national emergency,
With protective garments and headgear so difficult to work in and to see.

Two years of intermittent classroom attendance,
Distance teaching, distance learning, achievement by chance.
Face to face delivery, with debate, is essential,
Reaction, response, revealing pupils' potential.

Likewise, with GPs' patient diagnosis by telephone call,
Only 'face to face' should be provided for all,
To see the patient in the round, their colour,
Their temperature, blood pressure and demeanour.

Did furloughing staff offer a safety net,
Or create one enormous unexpected national debt?
Was our work ethic tarnished for ever,
Have we lost the desire to work together?

'Working from Home' is in debate,
Will folk return through the office gate.
Daily commuting all week long,
Or work at home, singing the latest song?

This bug revealed the folly of separation,
Confusing advice coming from each devolved administration.
A Germ War Cabinet with a single voice to us all
Is needed to establish any national virus 'firewall'.

We can all be wise after the event,
Let's just learn lessons on how to prevent.
It took courage to deal with this virus unknown,
Far more courage to repair what has been sown.

**000 - 000**

# A REVIEW OF COVID-19 - 2

## Its Impact on Towns

A drive around town on desolate streets,
Passing locked up shops, no chance of buying fruit or sweets.
A reminder of the '40s and '50s Good Friday observation,
Empty streets, closed shops, BBC's solemn music for the nation.

Two years of COVID has left its mark,
For many, confinement has killed their spark.
Keeping safe within four walls
Has created too many anxious souls.

Repetitive scenery with limited span,
From when this world-wide bug began.
Will this virus continue to mutate at will?
How many more humans will it kill?

Venturing out all masked up, metres apart,
Popular High Street stores have lost all heart,
Their shop-front names no longer displayed up high,
Locked up empty shells with memories of times gone by.

Now, as we emerge into a new environment,
Face masks, distance markers, to bins are sent.
Retail has made a major shift, no face to face,
On-line sales brought to your door at quite a pace.

Working from home with modern technology to hand,
No traffic delays, no commuting, no seats, just stand.
But this could be another form of Covid lockdown,
No office chat, no Company, nor company, sound.

Our towns and cities have lost their old contribution,
Delivering the breadth of services across our nation.
Just 'sample' retail of what's on-line,
and 'returns' to drop,
And Supermarket sheds, with their 'One Stop' shop,

Towns are changing to meet modern life and culture,
Their purpose, their role, creates a new picture.
Cosmopolitan life now developing in so many ways,
And the arrival of COVID hastened the pathways!

**000 - 000**

## DO AS I SAY, NOT AS I DO

A formal order from the highest command,
'Stay Safe' sent out to all, across the land.
Failing to obey your own command you will rue
The arms of the law on your shoulder will accrue.

Your authority is lost, so is trust,
An elevated status scorned and bust.
Hypocritical behaviour is all too common,
From political utterances to many a sermon.

COVID-19, an unprecedented form
of biological warfare,
What it is, and how to deal with this poisoned air.
Experts and scientists toiled for all their worth
To find a solution, to treat and protect us all
upon this earth.

To ignore their advice, the guidance was clear,
Foolhardy behaviour as they drank
their wine and beer.
Insulting to those who worked to protect us,
The millions who obeyed, fighting this virus.

This period of COVID-19 has been a strain,
Its consequences have given so many great pain.
Strict adherence to safety measures,
Sacrifice of love and simple pleasures.

Undermined by selfish, deliberate actions,
By those employed at the highest stations.
And many who defied the law and arranged to meet,
Self-interested, egoistic, in the open or discreet.

The rule of law applies to all,
It demands adherence; that is the call.
This virus was a challenge for all to fight,
To restore our freedom, and friendships reunite.

**000 -000**

# 2020

## Extracts from Institute for Government analysis.

| | |
|---|---|
| 16 March | PM - time for everyone to stop travelling. |
| 19 March | PM - UK can turn the tide in 12 weeks. |
| 23 March | PM - orders people to stay at home. |
| 26 March | Lockdown measures legally come into force. |
| 4 July | UK's first lockdown comes into force in Leicester. |
| 14 September | In England - Rule of Six. |
| 30 September | PM says UK at a 'Critical Moment'. |
| 5 November | Second national lockdown in England. |

# 2021

## Extracts from Institute for Government Analysis

6 January — England enters third lockdown.

22 January — PM publishes a roadmap for lifting the lockdown.

8 March — Recreation in outdoor public spaces allowed between two people.

29 March — Outdoor gatherings of either six people or two households will be allowed.

29 March — 'Stay at Home' ends but encouraged to stay local.

12 April — No indoor mixing between different households allowed.

17 May — 30 people only to mix outdoors, Rule of two or two households allowed for social gatherings. Indoor venues reopen. Up to 10,000 spectators can attend the very largest outdoor-seated venues.

14 June — Government accelerates the vaccination programme. Restrictions on weddings and funerals lifted.

24 July — Face coverings mandatory
Plan B to be used if the NHS comes under 'unsustainable pressure' and measure regarding face masks.

8 December — PM announces 'Plan B'; spread of Omicron variant.

10 December — Wearing of face masks becomes compulsory in most public indoor venues.

15 December — NHS COVID Pass becomes mandatory in specific settings.

# 2022

1 January. Official events to celebrate New Year were cancelled but crowds gathered to welcome in 2022.

New Year Honours to senior advisers to PM and senior Health Officers

3 January. Omicron variant continues to spread. Warning of staff absenteeism in schools and NHS.

5 January. 1 in 5 in the UK had COVID on New Year's Eve.

17 January. Rail companies operating emergency timetables due to high number of absentees

19 January. PM announces COVID passes at certain venues and events, and facemasks to cease after 26 January.

31 January. Restrictions for Care Homes are relaxed.

8 February. Health Secretary warns numbers will not begin to fall until 2024.

28 February. PM confirms all domestic COVID measures in England lifted from 24 February.

21 March. Spring Booster Programme launched.

7 April. Hospitals in England under 'enormous strain'

19 April. Patients waiting in NHS hospitals, GP surgeries, and A&E in England no longer required to socially distance.

**NB** Instructions differing in the other UK nations

# ACKNOWLEDGEMENT

The publication of this final book of the series, has only been possible with the help and support of others.

In particular, I am grateful to my son, Russell, (lobsterdm.co.uk) for the design of an excellent website, providing a means of publicising my books during lockdown. Not forgetting grandsons Olly Dodd of Wolly Productions for his local support and Ben Tattersall for 'putting words into my head'!

Finally, thanks to my wife and all my family and friends who have supported me from the start of this late-in-life new experience.

This world-wide pandemic has provided an unusual and unexpected stimulus, with many putting pen to paper, brush to canvas, and words to music. A small bright light in a world of sadness and confusion.

Stay safe.

Neil.

## BOOKS IN THIS SERIES

### BOOK 1

This unique book of over 30 reflective rhyming poems provides a personal contribution to the social history of the 20$^{th}$ Century growing up in a Welsh mining village during WW2.

### BOOK 2

This unique book of 30 rhyming poems provides personal observations on modern life, politics and the environment.

### BOOK 3

Another unique book of over 30 rhyming poems providing more contributions to the social history of the 20$^{th}$ Century, from WW2 to COVID – 19.

### BOOK 4

30 unique rhyming poems offering a contribution to the social history of the 20$^{th}$ Century and personal observations on modern life.

### BOOK 5

FORTY rhyming poems completes the author's personal contribution to the social history of the 20$^{th}$ Century and personal observations on modern life.

# POEMS BY AN OLD CODGER

## A series of five books

The author, who grew up during World War Two in a Welsh mining village on the outskirts of Wrexham, offers a unique, personal, contribution to the social history of the 20$^{th}$ Century. This series of five books of rhyming poems takes the reader through his war-time schooling, enduring blackouts as enemy aircraft flew overhead, rationing, the swinging 60's, the Cold War era and, finally, COVID-19 lockdown. There are poems on his village life, family mining tragedy, his military career as an Education Officer in the RAF, 'Tales from the Organ Stool' and many others.

The reflections on his life are balanced by his observations on modern life, politics, and the World Wide Web.

The series will not only prompt memories for the elderly but help younger readers realise how different the world has become over the author's lifetime.

For information on the author, please log on to his website -

**www.oldcodgersbook.co.uk**

Printed in Great Britain
by Amazon